TREETOPS

TIM...
CHRONIC...

The Stone of Destiny

Written by David Hunt
and illustrated by Alex Brychta

OXFORD
UNIVERSITY PRESS

OXFORD
UNIVERSITY PRESS

Great Clarendon Street, Oxford OX2 6DP, United Kingdom

Oxford University Press is a department of the University of Oxford.
It furthers the University's objective of excellence in research, scholarship,
and education by publishing worldwide. Oxford is a registered trade mark of Oxford University Press
in the UK and in certain other countries

Text written by David Hunt, based on the original characters created
by Roderick Hunt and Alex Brychta

First Edition published in 2012

British Library Cataloguing in Publication Data

Data available

ISBN: 978-0-19-8475705

10 9 8 7 6 5 4 3 2 1

Printed in China by Imago

Paper used in the production of this book is a natural, recyclable product
made from wood grown in sustainable forests. The manufacturing process
conforms to the environmental regulations of the country of origin.

Acknowledgements: The publisher and authors would like to thank the following for their permission to reproduce photographs and other copyright material:

P46 Alan King engraving/Alamy; TsR/Shutterstock; Valentin Agapov/Shutterstock; 19th era/Alamy; Creativ Studio Heinemann/Westend61/Corbis; **PP46-47** Jakub Krechowicz/Shutterstock; Denise Fortado/ Shutterstock; Blaz Kure/Shutterstock; **P47** Picsfive/Shutterstock; magicinfoto/Shutterstock; WildCountry/ Corbis; Iain Masterton/Alamy

Chapter 1

Rain lashed against the faces of the English soldiers. They stood looking at the small walled town, and they waited. Their king, Edward, stood between them and the town's walls. Though he spoke to his army, he knew the people in the town could hear him.

"A strong leader. That's what people need," King Edward shouted. "A king needs to be as hard as stone. Scotland has no such king.

Scotland's castles have crumbled before us. Scotland is ours."

At the flick of Edward's arm, a line of archers drew their long bows, the arrows aimed high into the sky above the town.

"The Scottish king is skulking behind those walls," cried Edward. "He is ready to give up. But before he does, let us remind him of the power a real king has."

The archers released their bowstrings. A swarm of arrows cut through the driving rain, high over the town.

From within the town, a thousand faces looked up as the flight of arrows passed overhead. Amongst them was an anxious king who nervously steadied his crown as he peered upwards. Everyone knew what the arrows meant. It was time for Scotland to give up its king.

The townspeople watched as the gates opened. Hidden within the crowd of faces, as the Scottish king stepped forward, were Chip and Kipper.

Chapter 2

Minutes earlier, Chip and Kipper had been with the others eating dinner by the fire in the library. Mortlock had made one of his 'special' stews.

"Um … interesting …" said Chip as he cautiously tried a forkful. "What's in it?"

"Bananas," smiled Mortlock.

Suddenly the TimeWeb alarm went off.

Wilf put down his plate. "Saved by the bell," he whispered.

Tyler looked worried. "This is serious," he murmured. "Two dark patches."

"So, that means two different Viran attacks, right?" gasped Biff.

Tyler nodded. "Both on the same thread of light. One in Scotland, one in England. But at two different points in history."

Wilf glanced at the globe next to the matrix. An image of a stone block with a metal ring at each end glowed dimly within it. "A block? What does that mean?"

"Not sure yet," said Tyler. "But we can't hang about trying to work it out. Two groups. Wilf and Biff, Chip and Kipper. Go! Now!"

Chapter 3

"King John of Scotland! Or perhaps I should just call you John. John Balliol. Kneel before your true king!" King Edward smirked. "The King of England!"

Slowly King John knelt down in the mud. Standing over him, King Edward began to laugh. "Pathetic!" he sneered. Some of the English soldiers began to jeer and mock.

Then Edward did something that made the onlookers in the town gasp in horror.

Ever so gently, Edward ran his hand over an embroidered badge stitched onto King John's robes.

"Scotland's Royal Coat of Arms," he murmured. "Such a shame!" His fingers dug down into the fine material. In one movement, Edward ripped the badge from King John's gown. The Scottish king fell backwards from the force, his crown landing heavily in the mud.

Somewhere at the back of the onlookers, Kipper was on his Link to Tyler. "I thought the English were supposed to be the good guys," he whispered.

Tyler's voice crackled from the Link. "Depends on who is writing the history," he said. "Anyway, I reckon there is no such thing as 'good guys' and 'bad guys'.

Sometimes people do good things, sometimes bad. The English are the same as everyone else."

King Edward was now standing on top of a wagon loaded with boxes. "People of Scotland," he shouted. "You have no need of any king but me." He held up the muddied crown that had fallen from King John's head. "Therefore you have no need of this crown." He tossed the crown into one of the boxes. "Nor do you need all the other

things I have gathered whilst toppling the castles throughout your miserable land. No need for your official documents any more!" From a box Edward grabbed a bundle of documents. "I have them all! Your records, your laws, and even your history! Like you, they all belong to England now."

An old man stepped from the crowd of townspeople. “O King! I am old and fear you not. So I will speak my mind. Once your army leaves our lands, we will write new laws. Even make a new Scottish king.”

“Do you think I hadn’t thought of that?” laughed the English king. He clambered to the end of the wagon. “But how can you crown a king when you no longer have this?” He pulled a cover to one side. Beneath, was a large, roughly hewn, block of stone. “I picked it up when I visited your Abbey in Scone. It’ll look nice in London!”

A shocked murmur rippled through the townspeople. “The Stone! He’s got the Stone of Scone!”

For a moment, the old man was lost for words. The sky seemed to darken and the rain drove down even harder.

Edward looked up, the rain dancing on his craggy face. “Don’t tell me!” he sneered. “The sky is weeping for Scotland!”

The old man found his voice. “O King. I warn you now. Do not take our Stone to England. Wherever it rests, a Scottish king will eventually rule. That is its destiny.”

King Edward’s piercing eyes fixed the old man. “England ruled by a Scottish king?” he growled. “That’ll be the day!”

Chapter 4

Tyler pressed the 'speak' button on his microphone. "Listen up, everyone. I've just spoken to Chip and Kipper. They're in 1296. They reckon they've just seen that block of stone we saw in the globe. I've done a bit of research. It seems that Scotland had a sacred stone that their kings sat upon to be crowned. I say 'had' because in 1296 King Edward the First stole it and took it to England. So, it might be that this stone, the 'Stone of Scone', is what the Virans are after."

From somewhere in history, Wilf answered. “Do you know what happened to this stone? Thing is, it could be anywhere, and right now so could we. Biff and I are in a huge church, at night, but we can’t tell at what point in time.”

“I’m trying to get a fix on you,” answered Tyler. His fingers typed frantically on the matrix as he talked. “As for the stone, King Edward had it placed under the English throne, and it stayed there for hundreds of years ... Hello? Wilf? Can you hear me?”

But all Tyler could hear was the hiss of deep history. The link to Wilf had been cut.

Chapter 5

Wilf snapped the Link shut. The noise of many distant footsteps echoed around the dark space.

"Quick, hide!" hissed Biff.

Behind an old stone tomb, they watched as candles were lit. In a criss-cross of long shadows, a group of men in dark cloaks walked towards them. Two of the men were carrying a wooden chest – a chest big enough to carry a large stone in, perhaps?

"Could they be Virans?" whispered Biff.

The men stopped opposite the old stone tomb. They stood around a finely carved wooden chair with a tall pointed back. Holding a candle, one of the men knelt down and peered beneath the throne. "I have waited many years to see this stone," he whispered. "And now here it is, in front of me."

Biff and Wilf tensed. Carefully, they pulled out their Zaptraps.

They held their breath as another of the men leant against the tomb. He patted its dusty lid. “Old King Edward wouldn’t be happy though, would he, eh?” he chuckled.

Without daring to move, Wilf strained his eyes to look at the tomb. Painted in gold letters along its marble side was an inscription: ‘The Tomb of King Edward the First, Hammer of the Scots.’

The man who had been kneeling stood up. “Shall we do this, gentlemen?” he said. The wooden chest was opened. Biff gripped her Zaptrap. She signalled to Wilf to stand by.

“I’ll make myself ready,” said another man, and he took off his black cloak to reveal a tunic of finely spun gold. He slowly sat down on the throne, and sighed. In the glow of the candles, his clothes seemed to shimmer majestically.

The other men revealed similar fine robes beneath their cloaks. Two of them looked like priests.

"What is going on?" murmured Wilf.

One of the priests spoke to the man sitting in the throne. "As you know, Sire, tonight is our last chance to practise the ceremony." He reached into the chest and pulled out a heavy gold crown. "Tomorrow is the day you will be crowned King of England!"

The man on the throne chuckled. "Who'd have thought it? Me, James the Sixth, King of Scotland, ruling over England!"

Chapter 6

There were books scattered all over the floor of the control room. Tyler had found a lot of information for Wilf and Biff. The trouble was, their Links had been switched off for some time. Frustrated, Tyler had tried Chip and Kipper instead.

"I've located Biff and Wilf. 1603. They're in London. Westminster Abbey. Near the river. And get this, you two! 1603 was the year Elizabeth the First died. She had no children, so England was out of a monarch!"

"What happened?" Chip's voice sounded fuzzy over the speaker.

"In a nutshell – Scotland! The Scottish king, James, became England's king too."

Despite the hiss from the speaker, Tyler heard Chip gasp. "So the old Scottish man was right. It *is* a Stone of Destiny! Wherever it ended up, a Scottish king would rule."

"Unless, perhaps, the Virans get involved," replied Tyler. "Be alert, you two. They want that stone. Why else would they attack two different points in time?"

Chapter 7

Under the rushing clouds of a stormy dawn, Chip and Kipper were forced to make a move.

The wagons carrying the stone, and the other Scottish treasures Edward had stolen, turned away from the town and headed south.

With their heads lowered against the freezing rain, none of the English wagon-drivers noticed as Chip and Kipper broke from the undergrowth and clambered over the side into one of the wagons.

Through forest and along cliff-tops, the line of wagons slowly jolted its way towards England. Chip and Kipper hid under the cover next to the stone. Nothing happened all day, except that they felt every rut and pothole the wagon went over. Nothing happened until dusk, that is.

Lulled by the rhythm of the wagon, for many hours the drivers hadn't even spoken. Then, suddenly, a cry of sheer terror broke the silence.

Above the wagon track, hanging upside down from the branches of a tree, were two enormous bats. At least, that's what they looked like. But surely no bat could be that big, could it? They were more like … men! Men in long black cloaks. But these were no ordinary men, as Chip knew only too well.

As two streaks of darkness, the Virans dropped on to the wagon next to the drivers. It was over in seconds. The Virans had control of the wagon and all that was in it.

With the oxen's reins gripped hard, the Virans let out a deafening hiss. Terrified by the sound, the oxen stampeded. The wagon lurched forward at speed. Chip and Kipper were thrown back, landing heavily against the stone. Within a moment their wagon had careered out of sight of the other wagons, as it headed towards the cliffs.

Not even the full force of the wind on the cliff-top seemed to slow the oxen down. Stunned, Chip and Kipper held on as the Virans drove the wagon on towards the edge of the cliff. With horror, Chip suddenly realized what was about to happen.

"Kipper! Zaptrap! Now!" Chip screamed. At the same moment both Virans leapt from the speeding wagon.

In mid-air, the Zaptrap's bright blue bolt of energy connected with one of the Virans. The Viran exploded into a whirling darkness. At the same time, one strand of the energy skimmed the side of the other Viran. As he landed on the ground, half of his human disguise was ripped away, the other half still in human form.

While this was happening, Chip threw himself forward and grabbed the reins.

As he pulled hard to one side, the wagon veered away from the cliff edge. But it was not enough. The oxen broke free as the back wheels went over the cliff. The wagon stopped, teetering over the edge.

Chapter 8

Even though King James and the other men had long gone, Wilf and Biff stayed hidden behind the tomb. “If the Virans are after this stone, this is where they’ll come,” Biff had told Tyler. “It’ll be tonight, we reckon. Before the coronation.” And so Biff and Wilf waited. And waited.

In the bitter cold of dawn, a voice jolted them awake. “I have heard from our leaders. The others have failed. Some Time Runners got in the way. It is down to us now!”

Two shadowy figures moved towards the throne, and knelt down. They began to pull the stone out from underneath it. Wilf nodded to Biff and they both stood up together, Zaptraps at the ready.

But these Virans were quick. Sensing movement from behind the tomb, they were ready. What is more, they had a surprise for the Time Runners – a new weapon.

In the split second before Biff and Wilf had a chance to aim their Zaptraps, both Virans had launched a ball of pure dark anti-energy from their hands. These globes of black mist whirled around Biff and Wilf, choking them inside a screaming darkness. It was no wonder the Virans had given them the name 'smotherspheres'.

By the time the darkness had cleared, the Virans were gone, and so was the stone.

The Virans had a plan, and so far it was working. The quickest and easiest way out of London was along the river. The Virans had moored a boat alongside some building works opposite the Abbey. Using the building site's wooden crane, the plan was to lower the stone over the side and on to the boat.

The stone was hanging high above the boat by the time Wilf and Biff spotted the Virans. At least, they spotted one of them.

He was lowering the stone down to the other Viran in the boat. With the Viran taking the strain, this time, it was the Time Runners' turn to have the element of surprise.

Wilf launched his Zaptrap. It zipped towards the Viran standing by the crane. As a blizzard of blue energy ripped through him, the Viran let go of the rope. The stone fell on to the waiting Viran below before it crashed through the boat and sank. By the time Biff and Wilf got to the river, there was nothing to see but a few pieces of smashed boat floating on the surface.

"Not our best moment," said Biff. "One Viran missing and the stone at the bottom of the river. We'll never be able to pull it up."

But Wilf had an idea. The other end of the crane's rope was tied around a block. "Help me push the block over the edge," said Wilf.

Using all their strength, little by little they eventually managed to topple the block over. Being slightly heavier than the stone, as the block sank, it pulled the stone up and out of the water. They had done it!

But something strange was happening to the stone. It seemed to be fading – almost disappearing. It was as if it were in danger of no longer existing. As if at some point in the past it was about to be destroyed.

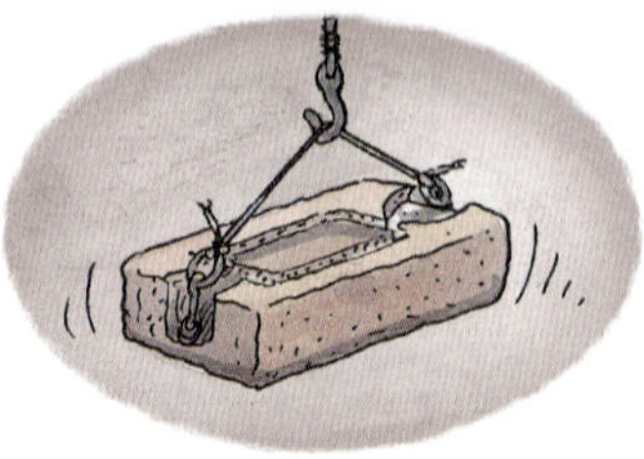

Chapter 9

Like a nightmarish seesaw, the wagon rocked slowly up and down on the edge of the cliff. Hanging over a raging sea, the stone had slid to the very end of the wagon. The only thing stopping it from falling off was Kipper. With a foot caught in one of the stone's rings he held on desperately to the side of the wagon.

Amongst boxes of papers, Chip sat at the other end of the wagon. He dared not move.

He was scared that if he did, he would change the weight that held the wagon in balance. If that happened, they would all tip over the cliff.

Gusts of wind whipped around them. The wind snatched at the boxes of documents. As more and more were blown into the air, the weight in the wagon slowly shifted. With heart-stopping creaks and groans, Chip's end gradually lifted whilst Kipper and the stone sank downwards. Neither of them knew what to do. "This might be it, Kipper," said Chip.

But Kipper had an idea. From the side of his Link he pulled out a long wire. Ever so gently he threaded it through the ring of the stone. Then he threw his Link to Chip.

Set back from the cliff was the edge of the forest. “See if you can hook the Link around a tree branch,” Kipper shouted. “Then jump. The wagon will fall away, but I’ll hold onto the wire. Hopefully it’ll hold both the stone and me. Do it! It’s our only hope.”

Chip was terrified. He couldn’t afford to get this wrong. With all his concentration he swung the Link back and forth harder and harder whilst he took aim. Choosing a ‘Y’ shaped fork in a sturdy looking branch he released the Link high into the air. But as he did so, the wagon juddered further over the edge. The Link fell short.

"Missed!" Chip cried. "It's no good, Kipper. I can't do it again. We'll all go over the edge." Chip and Kipper sat looking at each other. The situation looked bleak.

Then, suddenly, they heard a voice carried in the wind. A young Scottish girl had been watching them from the forest.

The girl picked up the Link and climbed a tree. She tied it firmly behind a branch. "Jump!" she shouted.

Chip leapt from the wagon. It gave another lurch and slid away over the edge. The wire held. Kipper and the stone were saved.

"I am sorry I didn't come out sooner," said the girl. "I thought you were English soldiers. My name's Alba." Alba nodded at the stone. "I watched them take that," she said.

"Are you going to take it back?" Chip asked.

"Nah! We'll survive! Let the English have it," Alba laughed. "Some people say it isn't even the real Stone of Scone. Edward was tricked. They say the real stone was hidden away and the one Edward stole was a fake. Some even say the stone he stole was actually a cover for a drain!"

Glossary

careered *(page 27)* To move or swerve wildly about. *Within a moment their wagon had careered out of sight ...*

destiny *(page 15)* Fate, or what the future holds. *"That is its destiny."*

juddered *(page 40)* To shake or move violently and noisily. *... the wagon juddered further over the edge.*

monarch *(page 23)* A ruler with a title such as king or queen, emperor or empress. *"She had no children, so England was out of a monarch!"*

sacred *(page 16)* Something that has spiritual meaning and so is very precious. *"It seems that Scotland had a sacred stone that their kings sat upon to be crowned."*

skulking *(page 4)* Hiding, or sneaking away in a time of danger. The word can carry a feeling of cowardly behaviour. *"The Scottish king is skulking behind those walls."*

Thesaurus: Another word for ...

skulking *(page 4)* lurking, loitering, sulking, hiding.

Tyler's Mission Report

Location:	Date:
Scotland / England.	1296 / 1603
Mission Status:	**Viran Status:**
Mostly successful.	1 zaptrapped. 2.5 zapped.

Notes: Some Virans still loose.

The idea of history is a hard thing to get your head round. We tend to think of things that happened as fixed. Like they are facts or something. And of course there are facts in history: names, dates, places and stuff. But if you think about it, history is mostly made up of people's experiences. And this is where it gets tricky. Two people might see the same event happening, but tell a very different story afterwards depending on how they felt about what happened.

The problem is that history only tends to remember the stories of those people who have the power to be heard. And usually they are on the winning side of whatever event they are writing about. In other words, history all depends on who is writing it.

Sign off: Tyler

Edward the First

History: downloaded!

Stone of Destiny

It is said that the Stone of Destiny came to Scotland from the Holy Lands many centuries ago. Whether that is fact or not, does not matter. To the Scottish people it represented Scotland itself – and its king, recognized by God. Scotland was a nation in its own right and not merely lands to be ruled by others.

Perhaps the Stone united the people in other ways too, through memories of the distant past. The ancient pagan tribes of Scotland believed their kings were married to the very stones they stood upon. To be a king, then, was to have a deep connection with the land itself.

But what was this land called Scotland? Where did it begin, where did it end? Who could claim they ruled it all when marshlands and lochs, highlands and islands, impossibly divided the land itself? The Romans had no idea. They simply built a wall of stone that marked the end of their world.

However if the landscape made Scotland impossible to conquer, it made it just as hard for the Scottish peoples to unite. Power in Scotland was more about what you claimed to be yours than what actually was yours. Inevitably, the loudest, most aggressive claim would come from Scotland's powerful neighbour, England, and its ruthless king, Edward the First, 'Hammer of the Scots'.

For more information, see the Time Chronicles website:
www.oxfordprimary.co.uk/timechronicles

A voice from history

My father was so proud of his country that when I was born, he gave me its name. Alba. That's Gaelic for Scotland. And at that time, we knew who we were. Scotland had borders, it had culture, it had religion, traditions, a line of kings, a history all its own.

Then Edward came along. He pretended to help us sort out who our next king was to be. But actually he wanted to take Scotland apart, stone by stone. He even fixed it so that no Scot with any power could stand up for the Scottish people.

But he underestimates us. Scottish people have spirit. And even if we don't have a king to protect us, we are quite able to protect ourselves. I hear rumours. I hear names. One in particular – a rebel called William Wallace. Look out for him.